Other Works

Urban Mythology
Ambrosia

VIGNETTES

VIGNETTES

ERIC KEIZER

Mighty Quill Books
Pittsburgh, PA

Poems © 2017 Eric Keizer
Cover photograph © 2015 A.M. Rycroft
Cover design © 2018 A.M. Rycroft
Edited by Daniel Santiago

This book is a work of fiction. Names, characters, places, incidents, and dialogues are drawn from the author's imagination.

All rights reserved. This book or any portion thereof may not be reproduced or used in any manner whatsoever without the express written permission of the publisher except for the use of brief quotations in a book review or scholarly journal.

First Printing: 2018

ISBN 978-1-7320013-1-2

Special discounts are available on quantity purchases. For details, contact the publisher by email at info@mightyquillbooks.com or at:

Mighty Quill Books
c/o Mighty, LLC.
370 Castle Shannon Blvd., 10366
Pittsburgh, PA 15234

The "M" and quill design is a trademark of Mighty Quill Books, a subsidiary of Mighty, LLC.

To Julie, for your love and support,
despite my shortcomings.
Thank you.

Table of Contents

Woodland/St.Ambrose	1
Angst	2
Beginnings	3
Breath, Wasted	4
Broken Summer	5
Campfire at Saylorville	6
Garden	7
Corn Dance	8
Court Ave., 1992	9
Dawn	11
Daydreamer Thursday	12
Diner	13
Distance	14
East of Des Moines	15
Evermore	16
Farmhouse Summer	17
Futility	18
Honor Guard	19

Goat Cheese Moon	20
Heroes	21
Industrial Loft	22
Ironic Toast	23
Lightning Crash	24
Loathe	25
Matins	26
Mist	27
Mojo	28
Winter	29
Vanish	30
Time.	31
Sunday, 5 AM	32
Sunday Drive	33
Sunday	34
July, 1977	35
The Sun and Moon	36
Summer Camp	37
Streams	38
Spring	40

Spring Moon	41
Spider	42
Solitude	44
6:17 A.M.	46
Sing	47
Pictures of You at the Reservoir	48
Ana	49
Sept. 29th	50
Scarlett	51
Sand.	53
Reeds of Grass	54
Warren County Bridge	55
g.o.d.	57
Embers	58
Labor Day	59
Muse's Ennui	60
Reluctant Hero	62
Eulogy for Fredericka	64
Soylent Sausage	65
For Veronica	67

6:45	69
Response to Henley's Invictus	71
Bather	73
Brevity	74
Fiction	76
Insomnia	77
Acknowledgements	79
About the Poet Eric Keizer	81

Introduction

Vignettes is a love letter, of sorts. My memories of the time I spent in Des Moines, Iowa during my undergrad studies influenced most of the pieces contained in this collection. While it's true that time colors our recollections of people, places, and events which transform us, I have to admit that it might just be possible I have embraced subjectivity throughout this book, rather than objectivity. How could I not embrace the wonders I experienced as a young man in the early 90s? It was, for me, an exciting time to be alive.

Both the city and the people of Des Moines made me feel like I was home. Few cities can compare to it. Few residents of any city are as welcoming and friendly to strangers. There is an air of greatness swirling down the broad lanes of University Avenue. Court Avenue nightlife rivals that of any major metropolitan destination, and grand old homes of Beaverdale hearken back to an era of prosperity and architectural mastery.

Des Moines was unique in that, despite its urban sprawl, there was magic in the untouched spaces just outside of the city limits. Development gave way to wide open prairielands, where one could imagine a westerly wind shaking wheat tassels and songbirds serenading covered wagons as pioneers made their way toward new beginnings. Endless blue skies rivaled the hues of any famous artist's palette. I spent many lazy afternoons on the banks of the Raccoon River, fishing with like-minded buddies, who dropped a line in the water as much for the camaraderie as for the possibility of actually catching a fish.

    I am proud to offer this collection of poems as a tribute to the enduring beauty of Des Moines and its residents.

VIGNETTES

Woodland/St. Ambrose

I lie beside your tombstone,
I breathe the fog of death.
I only feel my heart beat now,
I barely see my breath.
I search for somewhere placid,
I search for something true,
The greatest loss I've ever known,
Was when they buried you.
My heart still beats, but broken,
I have no words to speak,
I stay here, keeping vigil,
And cry at angel's feet.
I lie prostrate above you,
Remember all I miss,
I'd give my life, salvation,
For one last tender kiss.

Angst

Hallowed dreams just fade away,
Hollowed out by,
Halo wearing devils,
Taking samples of my id
Cut paper thin by rusted razors.
And you, freshly showered,
sufficiently caffeinated,
Reborn,
Wonder aloud about my angst.
The obtuse anxiety over,
Those ignoble and immoral,
Who have stolen
The content of a soul.

Beginnings

Seeing you,
Becomes desire,
Raw emotion laid bare,
And quivering.
Small child innocence,
About a first crush,
wells up from deep inside,
And flows.
White capped rapids,
Turbulent crashes,
Dashing wooden dreams on rocks,
Yet sustaining beauty.
Like flowers drinking healing spray,
mere inches from the shore,
enraptured by this gift of life,
Unafraid of swirling waters.
I swim uncharted, unfettered,
Unfurled,
Amazed at what I see, and yet,
I wonder at the mists which rise,
Veiled promises of calm ahead.

Breath, Wasted

I recall
Lavender fields,
Sweet soul kisses,
Tender mornings,
Dew-like sighs of babies' sleep,
Soft whispers upon the wind.
But I,
for lack of memory's light,
Forget how special she is,
Again.
I turn to find the ghost I knew,
Only semi-aware she's gone and yet,
I smell lilacs
And touch,
Reach for,
wind borne-fingertips,
Brushing softly as goose down,
Upon my wrinkled,
Furrowed brow.

Broken Summer

I notice you,
Butterfly like,
Alighting on the fence rail,
Straw dangling precariously from your lips,
Cowboy hat askew,
Boots in stark contrast,
To white cotton dress,
Embroidered.
You smile your crooked smile,
And I melt again,
Block of ice in mid-July sun.
But it's not real,
And you're not here.
A ghost,
Specter
Of perfect summers,
Moonlit strolls,
love making in the hayloft
As I turn a rusty barbed wire strand,
Piano wire taut,
My resolve lies broken at my feet,
I bleed and feed the dust below,
With no more strength to give.

Campfire at Saylorville

In heavy velvet darkness,
The campfire shines,
Highlighting the outline of your face,
Delicate and soft,
Whispered breezes and flower scents,
Warm hues of fire colored skin, ethereal
Magical.
I catch my breath, as you start to speak,
I see your soft, tender lips.
And blue sparkles
Of your eyes.
Golden hair,
Rapunzel homespun,
Lifts and curls,
As you laugh, melodic, lilting,
Robin song lovely.
In this perfect moment,
I stare in wondrous
Amazement,
At flame- halos above you,
And open my singing heart.

Garden

I took one last look,
Around the cloister,
Of your heart.
My catholic view diminished,
Narrowed,
By simple private,
Confessions.
My penance now,
My purgatory,
Your abbey lies in silence.
Weeping eyes find little solace,
And even less salvation,
As I partake of sacraments,
And pray to see Gethsemane.

Corn Dance

Breeze blown waves of emerald green
Sway to silent music
Carried on wind
Silken corn tassels bow, then dance
Blithely touch, and move away
To only touch each other again.
While crows land with disdainful eyes
On effigies in tattered clothes,
And then scold the dancers for being too close.
The green clad ears eagerly await
To share a golden surprise
While swaying on one stalky leg.

Court Ave., 1992

Orange and pink,
fading twilight skies,
Begrudgingly yield
To neon bathed night.
Coltrane,
Ellington,
take the A train,
Avoiding uptown girls,
While time-eating cancers,
Consume revenant souls.
Jack and Diane,
Drink ten dollar coffee,
Angst ridden, volatile.
Too scared to admit
they're afraid of loneliness,
Working their ways,
Around each other,
While they bleed and tremble,
Thoughtless,
Suffocating.
Melting ribbons of asphalt,
Curl up at the edges,
Needing a bright pink bow,

While toothless mouths gum,
Salvaged dumpster steaks,
Throngs of co-eds,
Pub-crawl their way home.

Dawn

Silent dawn breaks purple,
slowly fading embers
Pigtailed wisps of smoke,
Rises from the now cold hearth,
As I gather bedclothes to me.
Where you lay beside me,
Warm to touch, inviting,
Your perfume scented pillow,
I breathe deep, absorb your essence,
And peer through sleep glazed eyes
I cry out, amidst the rush,
Of heavy, velvet truth,
Only silence resounds so loud,
In this barren,
Granite chamber.

Daydreamer Thursday

Beside a farmer's forlorn stream,
among the sands of its time,
I lie awake, but lost inside,
the imagined world of you.
Crushed grass stains,
On heavy denim,
And a half smoked joint
Serve to mask the truth,
The reality you've given,
Bullfrogs croak a stern,
Sober warning,
Opposed to my intrusion, while I
Submit, and close my eyes,
Drinking in your soft warm breath.

Diner

She stood there,
Disenfranchised,
Disaffected,
disarming me with her smile.
White apron tightly tied,
As Mazzy Star blared
From tinny speakers above us,
And I faded into her, again.
Until this moment,
I never noticed one blue eye,
And one green eye,
Behind her black horn-rimmed glasses.
"The usual, Hon?"
I nodded my affirmation,
Both of her,
And the food.
As she turned to get the coffee pot,
I thought just how
Strange it was she left me.

Distance

Soft fog rises between the furrows,
The Earth exhales slowly.
An orange-dot sun sinks low,
Bidding good night to stars.
Luna rises, stretches,
Wiping sleep from dusty craters.
Sinners hurry to bolt wooden doors,
Before twilight descends, and carries
primal fears to hearts,
Both superstitious and timid.
Frigid February flurries float,
And I imagine you again,
Dancing on the sand.

East of Des Moines

Guns of filth,
Loaded, primed,
Take aim at children,
Pregnant with potential.
Lowriders malevolently cruise
through the streets,
Oblivious to the finer things,
And instead serve themselves
Up to Mammon.
Old black men,
On older folding chairs,
Guard barber shop front doors, and
Shake their heads together,
At young bucks throwing signs.
Dreaming of Mama's collard greens,
Black eyed peas, chitterlings,
For Sunday suppers when,
Drive-bys didn't yet exist.

Evermore

Latent night, with rushing gloom
Seals the fate of darkened room,
The flowers curl,
Wither away,
While ghosts live on
Another day.
I hold the yellowed picture close,
Raise a glass in empty toast,
To you, someone I never knew,
But loved as though
Your love was true.
Your sweet scent still lingers here,
Your voice still rings out,
Crystal clear.
Although I die some more each day,
Your vision never fades away.
You haunt me when
I hear your name,
In whispered tones,
In mortal pain.
A raven cries out,
From demon core,
"You shall love her evermore!"

Farmhouse Summer

A summer sweetness blows through my window,
Lilac and lavender infused lace
Frayed cotton cobwebs, yellowed by time,
As though each day were just the same.
There is subtle beauty here,
And restrained passion lingers,
While her gingham dress dries on the line.
Well- worn floorboards herald summer,
And respites of a thousand steps.
Dust motes dance in low angled beams,
While willows shake in anticipation.
She peacefully dreams in an old rocking chair,
As I drink lemonade in silence.

Futility

My kiln dried bones,
Lie disheveled,
Uncounted.
Spread like autumn leaves
Carpeting neat squares
Of concrete sidewalks:
Some hide in corners
of drugstore doorways,
Behind varnished, ancient
Aspen panels,
Time- worn and musty.
Subtle vignettes,
Easily forgotten ghosts,
Washed away ,
through staunch steel grates,
Embedded in a cold, hard street.

Honor Guard

A soft parade,
Goes marching by,
Dressed in many hues.
Single filed miscreants,
The lovelorn poets weep.
Murderers and thieves come calling,
Striking finger cymbals,
Dancing to,
Throbbing chests,
Weakened knees,
With general malaise
Towards broken tin soldiers,
Who proudly stand and salute,
The humble wounded souls.
Fried chicken fingers squeeze
Lemons in lemonade,
And aim for the sky in twenty-one gun
Salutes,
For the fallen.

Goat Cheese Moon

Singing bullfrogs serenade crickets,
Who reply with their own cantata,
As bullrushes sway gently,
Rhythmically ,
Unison driven,
As cool breezes raise
Softly delicate neck hairs.
Beneath a poked hole sky,
Curtained by clouds,
Of bleached- white cotton,
Beaded lampshade lumens,
You shine brightest against
a goat-cheese moon.
You beside me,
Become a nymph,
Playfully chasing fireflies.
Laughing like a child,
Freshly scrubbed and innocent,
Capturing glowing hearts.

Heroes

(must-reads while sitting beside the Raccoon River)

Shakespeare laid there writhing,
When he should have been at rest.
Thoreau was stuck at Walden,
But sent along his best.
Joyce and Keats were smoking,
On the porch with lemonade,
While de Cervantes tilted at
The windmills he had made.
Twain was marking water depths,
While Hemingway set sail.
Poe regaled all of us,
With his morbid raven's tale.
As I lie here in my bed,
And chase elusive sleep,
They're still alive,
Inside my mind's
Battlements and keep.

Industrial Loft

I lie beside your body,
I am awake, revived.
Jarred from sleep by traffic outside,
And sunshine Saturday morning..
With easels standing watch,
Guarding us while we slept,
Sentient sentinels in abstract,
Multi-colored jackets,
In stark contrast to
White painted walls,
and coffee stained mugs.
I turn and watch,
As you breathe deep,
Inhaling motes,
Atoms of dreams,
While I long to kiss you awake.

Ironic Toast

Potential is a fickle mistress,
Filled with love,
And bitter, hateful recrimination.
She teases homogenous,
Homogenized white bread into
Believing
Its destiny is greater than the sum of its parts,
Until one day,
It lies blackened,
With rigor mortised crusts,
Passively, tacitly
Accepting softened butter
And currant jam.

Lightning Crash

You are the dream,
I never dared to speak.
A specter,
Gossamer thin,
delicate spider-web,
Until the day you crashed,
Thunder- like,
Lightning storm strike,
Arcing through the sky.
Your eyes reveal so much
In your solitude,
Yet I see through,
Into your soul.
The beauty you create,
By the very breath you take,
Magical ear music,
Cymbals crashing,
Heart string strummed.
I hold you close,
Inside the wooden chest,
Where I hide jars of lightning.

Loathe

Bathed in the crimson sun,
Watching the caramel sky,
Couldn't see your shadow,
Yet again.
Missing you is the price I pay,
For loving a mere ghost,
Your dark heart is empty.
Mine is bursting.
I tread solemnly in
Quiet introspection,
Seeing but not retaining,
Feeling but not comprehending,
All the joy that you once gave,
Lies broken,
Bleeding,
Burn pile fuel,
Polluting October skies.
As tidal waves of remorse,
Self -doubt,
Become as droplets in this stream,
Of convoluted,
Brackish,
Romantic self- loathing.

Matins

Her sullen majesty awaits,
Whilst I stand naked to the
Wind,
Dripping down my rusty blood,
from spiraled daggers,
Molten.
Baby's breath—soft flowers
Adorn her golden ringlets of hair,
While gossamer strands float listlessly,
Painfully aware of how they'll catch
The jagged tears of skin
Surrounding when my heart once beat
She cradles love in ivory skinned hands,
Long elegant fingers,
Delicately wrapped,
Around her hoary prize,
As
I kneel in supplication,
Watching crimson travesties,
Reflect in her blue pools,
While cathedral bells,
And catechisms,
Summon all to matins.

Mist

Soft rain
Touches gently, on
Silken flower petals,
sways green leaves
In syncopated rhythm.
Staccato serenade,
Joyously exuberant,
Innocent in purpose,
Soft as mothers' love.
I watch as parched earth
Greedily drinks deep,
Sponging up the
Crystal spheres
Of my windborne
Longing.

Mojo

I fear my mojo's broken,
Or at the least,
Is lost.
I wanted luck in pleasure
But ended up like Faust.
I thought I spied a rabbit's foot,
A four-leafed clover there,
But now, it seems, it's striking deep,
My luck is off, somewhere.
The horseshoe that I found was bent,
The talisman was fake,
I fear before the Bacchanal,
I'll swim a fiery lake.
Oh, to live,
and think,
and dream about,
The worldly pleasure of man!
But in the end, it's clear to me,
I'm right where I began.

Winter

I stood among the browning weeds,
Leaves of grass
In fields
Plowed under and silent,
Barren
Life forces passing into winter,
Sparking lovesick dreams.
In my mind, a picture of you
Standing wearing white cotton
Blowing gentle kisses as you spoke
To me, in hushed whispers.
I heard your voice, and listened close,
Remembering each detail,
To lock away inside my heart,
Helping me survive,
A long cold winter,
Apart.

Vanish

The rain had come so softly,
Alighting on the sill.
The tear-shaped, little droplets,
Became a bitter pill.
I thought of how I loved you,
And dreams I had held fast,
But in this melancholy world,
Few dreams can ever last.
Whispered words on breezes,
Uttered in the night,
But by daybreak,
those tender words,
Vanished in the light.

Time.

Time,
In its inexorable
Crush,
Captures even the
Fleet of foot.
Slowly grinds
The joyous bones of youth
Beneath the
Sorrow of age.

Sunday, 5 AM

Gin.
Juniper berries.
The mystical jinn that makes up gin,
She giggled.
Three cigarettes,
Doubled over,
In exhaustion,
lying in their ash filled coffin,
While sunlight assails my eyes,
And I wonder,
Just who the hell she is beside me.

Sunday Drive

In Sunday dreams,
On gravel roads, I pass
Some fence pole groves.
While old men in their church clothes,
Broil in stiff backed pews.
Auxiliary ladies preen and strut,
Pecking at each other.
I downshift and silence,
Two tons of Detroit steel,
As I roll past the church where
We were to be married.
Big city voices shout aloud,
Through tinny AM speakers,
Telling me "The greatest of these…
Is love."
Salty tears meet salty sweat,
And streams on down my cheek,
As I run down the backroads,
Away from what I feel.

Sunday

Tranquility tiptoes in,
A stealthy mouse,
Cautiously moves past,
the sleeping cat of my mind.
While Sunday morning worlds
Rise to papers and coffee,
Well- worn dining tables,
And nearly dry muddy boots,
While gentle breezes rustle curtains,
sweep the windowsills clean.
I smell your perfume,
as you move through the kitchen,
unaware I know you're awake,
And smile in my soul,
For gracious gifts received.

July, 1977

Traveling in a '65,
Somewhere outside of Altoona,
The black dirt back roads,
Sharecropper shacks, and rusty
Shot up junk cars,
Shirtless little boys chase chickens with sticks,
and dogs laze about under creaky porches.
White-steepled churches,
And suit wearing black men,
In sweltering, oppressive heat.
The air inside is stale,
Hot.
This steel and glass behemoth.

The Sun and Moon

You are my Sun,
Golden, resplendent
Inside my kaleidoscope dreams.
I am your Moon,
I watch over you,
and bathe you while you sleep.
Enduring cold, and desolate skies,
I've felt the freezing wind
But you warm me in your heart,
And melt a frozen soul.
Sun and Moon, Wolf and Hawk,
And the twain shall not meet,
until the cleansing wind,
can wash away my sins,
Enrobing me in sacred light, ethereal,
Enveloping me in glory,
Reflected in your eyes.

Summer Camp

7Up bottle green,
Leaves dance in the breeze,
as west winds blow.
They cause a scene,
But move with ease,
Like pretty maids in a row.
Coyote nights
Meet sun bleached days,
In this world without an end.
Eternal fights,
Confused new ways,
leave hearts that cannot mend
After that luscious first kiss.

Streams

As lucid dreams,
Run through the streams,
Of consciousness,
I see their ebb and flow.
In daily dreams,
Of finer things,
I star in my own show.

But you stand there,
I am aware,
As loves remain and grow.
Parts of us are lost, it seems
In rapids, in their flow.

I love the way ,
That you see me.
I love your smile and laugh.
The way your dark heart replies,
Before I even ask.

And as I stare into the stream,
I watch as lives float past,

And think of how my life will be,
When I hold you close, at last.

For I am but a dreamer,
And you, the perfect dream,
We dance and sing,
And laugh and love,
In visions never seen.

Spring

She sings in sonnets,
Laughing through eyes,
Impetuous, mysterious imp.
Bereft of guile,
Devoid of guilt,
Devoted, devoted, devoted.
The May Queen dances,
Upon the heath,
Where hoary grass and grizzled
Blooms,
Recall the distant winter's grasp,
Our deathly paled,
and frozen moments,
Those who gasped beneath the crushing ice,
Are lost, save particles
On the breeze,
And whispered
Furtive promise.

Spring Moon

In just spring,
She is reborn, fertile
As newfound blooms reach for the sun,
She smiles.
She glows in green clothed splendor
While golden rays encircle her brow.
She awakens dormant passion,
And I kneel before her,
Infatuated, humbled
By all that she controls.
Her voice, melodious and clear,
Rings out across the field,
As if to call the still sleeping,
to behold her once again.

Spider

With silken strands,
The spider weaves,
A rivulet of thread,
While morning dew,
Sieves right through,
Baptizes her in bed.
She spins her tales,
Creates our past,
While Furies all ignite,
And burn for her,
In flames, azure,
Ablaze throughout the night.
She weaves the tales,
Of lovelorn men,
And suitors all aglow,
With heartfelt fire,
Impure desire,
She sadly, lets them go.
They are but flies,
Inside her web,
Insidious and strong,

And once they're snared,
They are prepared,
To vainly struggle on.

Solitude

My solitude in summer song,
Sings the swallow,
All day long.
In May's last gasp,
And June arrival,
Bleak winter's past,
And Spring's denial,
And bumblebees,
Who turn and dance,
With flower heads in silent trance,
Warm winds which blow,
The cobwebs out,
Charcoal rages at my doubt.
Butterflies, in dapper coats,
Assail the flowers of parade floats.
The Ice Cream man
with chiming song,
Patrols the village all week long.
Children laughing, skipping rope,
Bad brain freeze,
From root beer floats.

But I'm afraid I can't partake,
Of this world
I didn't make.

6:17 A.M.

My haggard eyes
Saw someone I don't know
Very well anymore,
In the steam tinged mirror
Again this morning.
Shaky hands shaved close,
To Adam's apple danger,
While whiskers washed away,
Clockwise,
And spiraling,
Down some dark rabbit hole.
I drank your coffee,
Ate your eggs,
As we talked of perfect ratios
Of butter to jelly on toast,
Anything to avoid
The inevitable
Goodbye.

Sing

I sing a song of virility,
And sometimes, one of pain.
I sing of love and brotherhood,
And pride besmirched by shame.
I sing of January's chill,
And crystals in the air,
Of February's sullen gloom,
For loves who are not there.
I sing of dreams and newfound love,
And March's springtime rain.
Of April's showers and fresh cut flowers,
May's amber waves of grain.
I sing about the girls of June,
All dressed in July's clothes,
About the leaves and shorter days
When wind in August blows.
I sing September's song for you
I sing October to your soul,
So when I'm in November arms,
December's gifts will glow.

Pictures of You at the Reservoir

The image of your face,
Is never far behind the lens,
Inside of my mind's eye.
In watercolors,
Which seep behind,
The canvas of my soul,
You sing and dance,
And love,
In exposed exposures.
My sepia colored memories,
Fade off time worn paper,
Yet you glide,
Elegant,
Effortlessly,
Frame by frame,
Print by print,
Life imitating art.

Ana

She is soft
Like a summertime butterfly wing,
Floating between roses and daffodils,
While the sweet breath of
a gentle westward wind
Blows dust across the prairie.
She comes to me in quiet dreams
Tenderly kisses my brow,
And I,
Unaware she leaves at dawn,
Remember nothing but lullaby songs.

Sept. 29th

In
Late
September,
When trees shake off
Their summer coats,
And blooms do fade away,
Singing children,
School bus bound,
Breathe deep as
Smoldering leaves
leave lazy wisps,
Curling smoky air.
You're born anew,
refreshed, untainted,
Gazing at pumpkin fields,
Warm apple cider eyes,
Cinnamon scented kisses,
I want to lie down,
Under the first snowy blanket,
And sleep inside your love.

Scarlett

Scarlett's heart lies broken,
while Rhett goes off to war,
and churches chime a sullen dirge,
because they love no more.

You are of the prairie,
And I am desert bred,
I love you so purely,
you say it's in my head.

though I am not with you,
for mountains in the way,
I am unsure of how to live
it changes day by day.

In summer skies I see you,
sparkling by the shore,
in winter's chill I lie alone
and long forevermore.

You are the Belle of Ankeny,
a lady, highly bred,
and I am truly but a fool,
who can't escape his head.

Sand.

Hourglass time,
Sands of fate, slowly move,
Implacable in silence.
You still remain a mystery,
Although I hear your voice,
everywhere.
You can't see the darker side,
The thoughts of shifting deserts,
Barren, vast,
Immovable
The Giza in my soul.
I run across the burning ground,
While you shift beneath my feet,
And leave me thirsting
For your touch,
While my eternity creeps forward,
grain by grain,
Burrowing in the crevices
Of my craggy face,
Burying me, shoulder high,
and exasperated, at the
Non-emotive,
And faceless.

Reeds of Grass

Reeds of grass stand bent,
With tired hunched up shoulders,
As old hay loft doors swing,
Jarringly open.
Gray grain silos point to heaven,
Exhorting me to fly to you,
But this land is in my soul.
Southern stars light nighttime paths,
For westward winds to knock at my door,
rousing ancient, leaded windows,
And grab for tenuous handholds,
At the ramparts of my heart.
How then should I,
Describe the longing
This duality presents to me,
The love of earth and land unbroken,
Or the dreams of future you?

Warren County Bridge

There's a bridge in Warren County that is burning,
It's been pretty broken up for years
Tonight the smoldering sparks turned into fire,
Can't be put out by a flood of tears.

Everybody says they saw it coming.
Rumored lies adding fuel to the fire
Breaking hearts that once burned for each other
Turn to ashes along with our desire.

The Warren County Bridge is falling down
Burns to cinders on the ground
Hopes and dreams rise in clouds of smoke
As we stumble and we choke
With stinging eyes and heavy hearts
We watch the flames burn up our parts,
As the Warren County Bridge comes falling down.

The firemen, in all their gear
Step back from the flames in fear
It's too late, we're too far gone
All that's left is to carry on.

g.o.d.

And maybe God really does mean,
Good orderly direction,
But not for downward spirals, vortices and whirlpools,
And tornadoes in my head.
Storms of rage and deceit,
Shrinking from lights,
But in dismal finality-
Acceptance
Because it's all futile
Puerile,
And hindsight is a bitch.
Sins aren't forgiven,
Just catalogued and
Pressed into moist skin
Like brands on
Doe eyed innocents,
Tallied just before slaughter.

Embers

Time steals embers,
Like naked Prometheus,
Frantic and anxiety ridden
Sprinting across mountain sides,
And verdant fields
Of lush passions,
And sodden memories.
Where tears extinguish
Faint smiles,
Scant promises,
But
Exacerbate chain-bouldered pain.
There's no Herculean tasks here,
Save
Regenerating hearts Harpies pluck out,
Nightly,
Eternally.

Labor Day

I knew you'd been there;
I could smell your perfume,
Saw stardust lined stairwell bannisters,
And remnants of a blue- plate lunch,
Only half eaten,
(a loft castoff)
Because diner stools are too high and
uncomfortable,
constricting (you lied)
Like how my chest tightens,
Breath escapes,
And I
Melt,
Become molten pools
Of plasma and regret,
When sleepless eyes land
On you,
Turtle neck sweatered,
And radiant
On a
Singular, momentous
Lincoln Park autumn
Tuesday.

Muse's Ennui

My inky diaspora,
(for words became my religion)
Preceded solely by
Exasperation for preventing
A mass exodus
Of ephemeral, fleeting,
Tenuous finger-tipped and
White knuckled flailing,
Failing grasps
At gasping utterances-
Tiny visions of ghosts,
Vapors
And mottled camouflage
Dappled in twilight remembrances
And still gasping for breath.
Awaiting me to breathe life into:
Diaphanous veils,
Where my lips won't form
Nascent probabilities,
Or pregnant pauses of potential.
Instead,
They beg for freedom,
From isolation and

Singular, insulated
Solitude,
But she,
Haughty and condescending,
Laughs at their pleas, turns a
Silken and cold shoulder,
Smokes a whale bone pipe,
And feigns disinterest.

Reluctant Hero

Our eyes met
Just above my raised newspaper,
A Zorro mask hiding
A wrinkled half face
(with half wrinkled skin).
And she was lovely,
A senorita in distress,
At not knowing the difference between
A grande and a venti.
But barristas are grouchy when
Theentiregoddamncityshowsupatonceforgoddamn
coffee
On their way to mass
Or to see the alcalde en el centro, anyway.
And so she stood,
Firing squad rigid and proud,
Not even needing a blindfold
(but maybe a cigarette)
when the count began.
I watched, silently observing from corner ramparts,
Wondering if I should
Swing down into the fray,
On a conveniently placed rope,

Reveal my rapier
Wit,
Or wait until
The garrison shuffled off to bed,
And whether,
If ,
I even could silence my own butterflies.

Eulogy for Fredericka

All hail Queen Fredericka!
Monarch butterfly killer and,
Monarch of an impromptu pond,
pooling just east of Peace Rd.
("The Barber Greene Lake" we jokingly
named it.)
But fair Fredericka,
Spawner of thousands,
Mother to none,
Abdicated her rush-y throne,
Perhaps because she was the bully-est of
All bullfrogs and frogettes,
And decimator of mosquitos,
And wanted to see why chickens got all of the
attention.
Now she lies, rigor-mortised and broasting,
One rigid pogo- stick leg raised
In Rockette- bare salute to traffic,
Struck down in her prime-of-life,
While her offspring croak their mournful calls,
And one stealthy fox lips her lips,
Awaiting nightfall and a free meal.

Soylent Sausage

His manners,
Impeccable.
A softly chiding,
"No elbows resting on white linen,
Mr. Rudnick!"
Alit, butterfly soft on a distant,
Receding memory of times long past.
Utensils arranged,
As Miss Yeardley's finishing school dictated.
A small jar of
Stone ground, artisanal, sherried mustard
Just beyond a gold- rimmed plate edge.
Oaken bouquet Burgundy swirled,
Blood crimson over an eager tongue,
As he thought of her.
Her sparkling eyes,
Golden hair,
And how she vowed she'd never leave,
Until she did.
He swirled,
Garlic mashed potatoes over
A mustard coated sausage slice,
Chewed her memory,

Swallowed any hint of regret,
Thinking,
How delicious her life had been.

For Veronica

She spied
Two blue herons
Fishing
From her
Riverbank river rock
Vantage point,
and wondered
Just what the big deal was,
Or who would miss her
If she slipped down, and drifted out to sea.
I'd see her
From a half- opened window,
And imagine
I could be her rock,
Arms to hold her above the surface,
Her heron,
Hero.
But I let cigarettes burn too low,
Singed my fingers,
And heavily sat
Rodin's Thinker-like,
in front of flapping curtains,
Behind walls I had built,

Immobile, unmoved,
Unaware she moved on,
Back home for dinner in
A silent grotto.

6:45

Harried mothers, unshaved fathers
Have washed tiny hands and faces,
Dried the last of dinner's dishes,
Retreated into inner sanctums,
As twilight softly gathers.
There's no sense of urgency,
For Friday's nearly asleep
And Saturday morning is
Still twelve hours away.
My deck light flickers,
Trying to caffeinate itself,
Like a Motel 6 beacon
For moths and fireflies
And those rotten mosquitos.
But I don't worry,
My single malt whiskey is smooth,
and cold
And outside of my glass pools condensation.
My deck is weathered and gray,
Like my beard and hair and eyes,
And I blend,
Monochromatic into pines and maples,
And contemplate

Sky, moon, stars, and childlessness,
frailty of age,
and the love of a sleeping dog.

Response to Henley's Invictus

I
We were fed
shit sandwiches,
Crusts intact, and all.
We listened to their pedagogies,
Ideologies,
Political furies,
In plastic- fantastic manufactured
Homesandcarsandcommunitiesandsocialconstructs,
Until there wasn't any place left to hide.
Overkilled warm butter brains,
Shredded by searing chainsaw
Executioners.

II
Talking heads,
Goose-stepping, spoon- fed automatons
Chant in unison,
"Consume all; trust us."
"Consume all; trust us."
"Trust us."

"For,
We know what's best for you."
Rich baritone, hypnotic frequencies,
Staccato drumbeat natives playing for
Oligarchies and overlords whose,
Details lie deep inside the devil.

III
And we cautiously tread through the Valley,
Became
afraid of the shadows,
of failure,
Of not-keeping-up-with-the- Joneses,
And the death-knell of simplicity,
Anonymity,
Laboring,
clamoring for elusive prosperity
we were taught to worship,
Until indoctrination
beat us into submission,
and we no longer felt
or questioned
or thought
for ourselves.

Bather

She bathed as I read aloud,
A barely restrained Sexton pouring,
Out from dually controlled spigots
Of melancholia and hopelessness,
Poured over bright enamel stuccoed dams,
Constrained only by a chrome stopper and,
Fear of what lies beyond.
And despite a faux beard of bubbles
And small glimpse appraisals of shapely calves,
Breaching surface tensions of
Waters and minds,
She
Wondered aloud about
Futility and
Recognizing one another
In whatever afterlife we find.
I closed the book; she flicked her ash
We contemplated vanilla scented silence.

Brevity

Is hard to maintain when
you're a twenty-seven-year-old ex-pat
exiled to your own back yard,
but you met her anyway,
and dinner and drinks were great
and she took your hand
as you strolled down Michigan avenue,
and you complimented her taste in music
and literature
and secretly
complimented her looks inside your mind
because you want her to know that you're not
some shallow sycophant who just wants to sleep
with her,
while you wonder if
she could actually be the one,
and your split consciousness listens,
really listens to her aspirations
because she's not some vapid shallow sycophant
who just wants to sleep with you,
and you hold the bar's door open for her
because
you're still old-fashioned

have respect and manners,
not because you feel like she can't do it for
herself,
and she smiles and thanks you and
again you notice her dazzling smile,
and the way her eyes flash when she talks about
Degas and her semester abroad 8 years ago,
and she says her cat's a jerk,
you both laugh and finish your drinks,
so you climb into the backseat
of some guy's cab,
and you tell him to wait while you kiss her
on her Wrigleyville's brownstone's steps,
the night air is magical,
and your cabbie smiles in his rearview mirror,
approving of her understated beauty
while you think to yourself,
"Brother, if you only knew."

Fiction

One yellowed bulb,
Highlighting yellowed,
Faded paint,
your cat (who never liked me anyway)
&
Grease splatters I missed,
While cleaning last week.

Those fictions we took for granted,
Stormed downstairs with you,
Piled in your backseat,
Gave me the finger,
&
Laughed aloud while,
Tail lights faded away.

And maybe I'm just revising,
editing fictions
where I'm Hector,
who treated you kindly,
&
Still couldn't stop wars inside your head,
during this three year campaign.

Insomnia

Wolves came howling
Around my front door,
From forests and gullies,
Barren spaces and jacked-up suburbs,
And I listened and wept
For the sadness in their songs,
For they never found out
If their mates ever heard.
I stalked a darkened
Biograph,
Cubby Bear,
&
Music Box.
I whispered for you to come out,
so we might prowl in tandem,
and I howled at full moons
and screamed,
foaming at L train clatter,
nearly drowned in between
green painted dumpsters,
when I couldn't run
anymore,
and the rain didn't let up.

I snapped at onlookers,
bared my fangs,
and growled,
but still they came,
in droves, in packs,
and I never once caught your scent,
or thought I saw you running,
so I stuck to shadows.
Once, I thought I heard you crying,
In that park across from Cardinal George's mansion,
But it was just a homeless woman,
softly singing herself to sleep.

Acknowledgements

Thank you, A.M. Rycroft and Erin Sloan for your vision, your friendship, and for believing in my work.

Thank you, Sam DeLoach for pushing me to grow and explore as a writer.

About the Poet
Eric Keizer

Eric was born and raised in Chicago. He earned his B.A. in English from Drake University, and his M.Ed. from Aurora University. He lives in northern Illinois with his wife Julie, and his dog, Edith.

Keizer's first published work was a short story included in an anthology. Since then, he has had one solo collection of poetry, *Urban Mythology* (2017), an anthology with eight other poets, *Ambrosia* (2017), and his latest, *Vignettes.*